D0712789

What Is Density?

By Joanne Barkan

Subject Consultant
Andrew Fraknoi
Chair, Astronomy Program
Foothill College
Los Altos Hills, California

Reading Consultant
Cecilia Minden–Cupp, PhD
Former Director of the Language and Literacy Program
Harvard Graduate School of Education
Cambridge, Massachusetts

Children's Press®
A Division of Scholastic Inc.
New York   Toronto   London   Auckland   Sydney
Mexico City   New Delhi   Hong Kong
Danbury, Connecticut

Designer: Herman Adler Design
Photo Researcher: Caroline Anderson
The photo on the cover shows colorful balloons.

Library of Congress Cataloging-in-Publication Data

Barkan, Joanne.
 What is density? / by Joanne Barkan.
  p. cm. — (Rookie Read-About Science)
 Includes index.
 ISBN 0-516-23618-0 (lib. bdg.)   0-516-24660-7 (pbk.)
 1. Matter—Properties—Juvenile literature. 2. Specific gravity—Juvenile
literature. I. Title. II. Series.
 QC173.36.B37 2006
 531'.14 — dc22
                                        2005021641

CHILDREN'S PRESS, and ROOKIE READ-ABOUT®,
and associated logos are trademarks and/or registered trademarks
of Scholastic Library Publishing. SCHOLASTIC and associated logos
are trademarks and/or registered trademarks of Scholastic Inc.
2 3 4 5 6 7 8 9 10 R 15 14 13 12 11 10 09 08 07   62

Knock, knock.
"Who's there?"

3

"Surprise!"

Six friends walk into
the room.

"Happy birthday!"
they shout. "This is a
surprise party!"

The room is much
more crowded now.
Do you know why?

At first, there was just one person in the room. Now there are seven people in the same room.

The density of people in the room is higher. Density measures how much of something is in a certain space.

Mom, Dad, and one sister bring in a birthday cake. Now there are ten people in the room. The density of people is even higher.

There is ice cream to go with the cake. The ice cream has chocolate chips in it.

Add a hundred more chips to the ice cream. Now the density of chocolate chips is higher. Why? There are more chips in the same amount of ice cream. Mmm, it tastes even better!

14

Everything is made of matter. People are made of matter. Cake and ice cream are made of matter. So are birthday candles and balloons.

Look at this popcorn ball. It is the same size as a baseball. But a baseball is much heavier than a popcorn ball. How can that be?

A baseball is made of matter. So is a popcorn ball. But the baseball has more matter in the same amount of space. That makes the baseball denser.

When two things are the same size, the denser one is heavier.

Watch the bubbles in a glass of orange soda. Why do they rise to the top?

21

22

The bubbles have less density than the soda. This makes them lighter. Up they go! Pop!

Oops! Someone let go of a balloon.

Why does it float up to the ceiling?

The balloon is filled with a gas. This gas has less density than air and is lighter.

So hold on to that balloon's string!

There are many examples of density at a birthday party.

Can you find other examples of density at home or school? You may be surprised by how many you find!

Words You Know

balloon

baseball

bubbles

popcorn ball   soda

31

Index

About the Author

Joanne Barkan is a science writer. Her book about fireflies and other creatures that glow has won awards from the National Science Teachers' Association, the Children's Book Council, and Parents' Choice. Joanne lives part-time in New York City, where the density of people is high, and part-time on Cape Cod, where the density of people is low.

Photo Credits